classical guitar student's Library

concert collection

CONTENTS

15-2-345

First Published 1986
International Music Publications

Exclusive Distributors
International Music Publications
Southend Road, Woodford Green,
Essex IG8 8HN, England.

Printed in England by JB Offset (Marks Tey) Limited
Marks Tey, Essex.

4.50

2

INTRODUCTION

Here I have selected a collection of Classical Guitar Solos, from which an interesting and varied programme can be compiled!

Some pieces are showy without being difficult, while others will allow the performer to add his own personal interpretation.

Many of the pieces are quite well known, while others are less familiar but have a useful place on the concert platform.

Pages 10 - 11

LUYS DE NARVAEZ. 16th centuary Spanish vihuelist. Exact date of birth unknown.

He came from Granada and had the reputation of possessing outstanding skill on his instrument. Narvaez published a book of tablature entitled "LES SEYS LIBROS DEL DELPHIN DE MUSICA EN CIFRA PARA VIHUELA" (Valladolid 1538) and introduced into Spanish music the principle of Variations, Guardame Las Vacas is an example of a theme and variations.

In the building of a programme, Guardame makes a very suitable opening number; it is well known and does not tax the technical ability of the player or the ear of the listener. Nevertheless, a good performance requires smooth melodic phrases, sustained bass notes, precise tempo and variations of tone. It is set here in 3/4 time and should be played at a tempo of about $\downarrow$ = 86 depending on the ability and temperament of the player.

The 8 bar theme is repeated harmonically but with melodic variations. The first variation consists of semiquaver note runs which should generate more movement but at the same tempo. The next variation has two moods: first the bass notes acting as a 'jumping-off ground,' and the second half a variation of the faster melody which ends with a graceful counterpoint finish.

The last variation is again in contrasting style employing bass to treble runs plus an extra 4 bars in thirds before ending on strong chords leading to an octave.

Pages 12 - 18

GASPAR SANZ was the most notable Spanish guitarist of the 17th century. He was born in Calanda, Aragon, and died at the beginning of the 18th century.

Sanz published three books of guitar music: the first in 1674, another in 1675 and the third (which included the previous two works) in 1697 under the original title "INSTRUCTION DE MUSICA SOBRA GUITARRA ESPANOLA" and a facsimile edition (dated 1966) was published in Zaragoza from which I have selected 'Canarios' and 'Passacalle.'

'Españoleta' should be played like a dance in a fairly fast three with a light lift. The grace notes must be carefully executed so that the first grace note is played on the beat together with the bass note as in the first full bar.

not before the beat

correct

incorrect

Only in the 37th bar should the grace note (with a line through it) be played before the beat, thus

but the grace note of the second beat which has no line through the stem must be played on the beat. Always sustain the bass note or any which sustain during movement of other notes within the phrase.

Bars 7 and 8 are generally written as one bar, viz;

and bars 15 and 16 as one bar, viz:

but in this version they are extended by lengthening the first note and thus adding a whole bar each time.

Canarios.

The Canarios is a dance rhythm and tune originating, as you may have guessed, in the Canaries. It is a jolly dance, effectively to be played at ♩ = 126 or thereabouts. The right hand work is of great importance and one must try to settle on a routine of picking. Generally it is in 6/8 rhythm but occasionally a strong 3/4 beat prevails which provides a very rhythmic contrast.

From the 29th bar there are fast appogiaturas or double grace notes occuring during the playing of two notes in harmony, so allow the top (melody) note to sound clearly while keeping the grace notes running.

It would be advisable to master the 'thirds' alone at first before attempting the grace notes which eventually should increase the excitement generated by a Canarios.

Passacalle.

After a 4 bar introduction sedately marking time, the melody commences with a 2 note lead in continuing for 16 bars. Make sure that the strong melody line is clearly stated before continuing with the straightforward variations, not forgetting light and shade.

J. S. BACH (1685-1750)   Pages 19 - 20

This Largo is the second and slow movement from the Concerto which is originally in F minor it has often been requested by guitarists.

I have deliberately set the tempo ♪ = 72 so as to give a regulator of eighth notes from which the length of the other notes can be measured. At first glance there seems to be a wild abundance of notes to cram into a bar, but really, it is not that fearsome. Imagine it written with a regulator, (i.e. beats) in quarter notes (crotchets) and it would look much easier.

Many of the fast runs are grace notes so the first thing to do is to establish the powerful melody then add the bass notes which you will soon discover are very regular. Providing you can play the bass notes at a steady beat, the melody and grace notes will fall into line. Take particualr care with the fingering in the correct positions on the fingerboard and it will all be possible.

JOHN DOWLAND (1563-1626)   Pages 21 - 23

Although, historically, this Galliard was written at an earlier period than the Sanz works, it never-theless seems a suitable follow-up to the previous music and at the same time provides a contrast in melody and style. Furthermore, it is technically a little more taxing.

This is taken from the collection "VARIETE OF LUTE LESSONS" by John Dowland's son Robert, and the original facsimile tablature contains 44 bars more than this version. I omitted part of the last variation partly because of space and partly to retain the interest of the player since there are long scale-like passages rather than instantly recognisable melody.

The sixth string of the guitar should be tuned to D and the whole should commence gracefully with the chords (where written fully) ringing through when playing the first eight bar theme. The second theme in the key of F is an echo of the first theme for 8 bars after which a 4 bar link is repeated bringing the subject to a conclusion, then returning to the original key of D major and continuing with this variation, following the basic harmonies. At this point there is a cut of 44 bars, of the third variation, picking it up at 4 bars from the end and finishing in D major in the last fascinating bar, but take care to use the correct fingering in order to sustain the last F♯ against the A and so ending in D major.

ALONSO MUDARRA (1546)

Although 'Fantasia' was also written in the 16th century I have placed it in a later position in the programme than the pieces by Sanz and Dowland because if played correctly and with the correct syncopation, it will sound more exciting than the previous pieces.

The composer writes "It is difficult until it is properly understood." and adds a footnote after bar 62, "From here on to the end there are some false notes. When played well they do not sound bad." One should listen to recordings by players like Alirio Diaz or John Williams to appreciate the harp-like phrasing.

There are probably a number of ways to finger the harp-like section and different guitarists have their own individual ways. However, the importance is to finger these sections as marked and to stick to the fingering until it becomes automatic. Of equal importance is the right hand picking which should flow. The only way to arrive at this stage is by repetitious practise at a reasonable tempo during which the brain is able to direct both hands in their diverse actions. Most players slow the tempo slightly from the 62nd bar onwards.

ROBERT DE VISSE (1650-1733 c.)

Robert de Visse was a French lutenist who played the guitar and theorbo and also sang for the Dauphin in 1686 serving as a Chamber musician to the King until 1721. He published a "LIVRE DE GUITTARRE" dedicated to the King in 1682 and another in 1686.

Here I have included the Prelude, Sarabande, Bourree and Menuet 2, all of which have been popular in our time and have been performed regularly.

At first, play the simple grace notes but when thoroughly familiar with the idiom, you should develop the grace notes and the mordants in the style of the era. There are really no problems other than holding the sustaining notes while changing a harmony note at the end of bar 3 and beginning of bar 4 of the Bourree where the F in the melody must be sustained while the G in the bass changes to A. There are a number of places in the Sarabande where the bass note sustains while the melody moves.

These suspensions are of extreme importance and the required notes should be held on. This is a general rule in producing correct phrasing.

FERNANDO SOR (1780-1839)   Pages 30 - 38

In my recently published "CLASSICAL COLLECTION OF GUITAR PIECES" I included a number of short pieces by this most prolific and excellent guitarist-composer who set the standard for the period, and here I have added concert pieces often included in Segovia's recitals. They make a contrasting selection eminently suitable for any recital. Furthermore, they present little difficulty to the student performer.

The Menuet is particularly straightforward, here, fingered by Miguel Llobet. He was rather fond of exaggerating apportamentos or slides, as, for example, in bar 12. Otherwise it is marked very clearly.

Andante Largo (in which the sixth string is tuned to D) is not as fast as it appears at first hand, so despite the time signature of 2/4 play it at the slow pace of $\flat$ = 92 or thereabouts, giving each quaver its full value, thereby allowing the melody to sing. The run of six demisemiquavers in bar 3 is much easier than it appears because the run is played by one pick of the fingers and a long legato from the left hand.

In the second movement, study the fingerings very carefully before you tackle the fast runs. This piece is often performed and has been recorded by leading guitarists so there should be no difficulty in hearing it performed correctly.

The Rondo makes a good finish to this selection of three Sor pieces and at the correct tempo makes a good finish to the first half of the programme. Technically, it demands a fair amount of left hand finger independence.

MATTEO CARCASSI (1792-1853)   Pages 39 - 41

This attractive tune in the Carcassi collection immediately strikes a familiar note, reminiscent of the 'Rondo' near the end of Rossini's opera "La Cenerantola". Technically, it poses no problems and the variations are in the style of the period and provide good practice for the right hand, good legato practice in the first variation and a turn of speed in the second variation which repeats for 8 bars before taking the second time bar and on to the end.

It should be played at a comfortable tempo ending with as much 'bravura' as possible.

JULIAN GAVINADE DE ARCAS LACAL (1832-1882)
Pages 42 - 49

During his lifetime he was considered the leading guitarist in Spain. He gave many concerts and wrote a large number of compositions for the guitar. He is also known for his decisive influence on Antonio de Torres the Luthier of Almeria and particularly on the design of the sounding board which Torres altered on the advice of Arcas.

Arcas was taken ill with a heart attack at the end of a concert tour which included Malaga and Antiquera and died three days later in his fiftieth year, His music is almost unknown to present day guitarists and I select Punto de la Habana not just because it is mentioned in Domingo Prat's Diccionaria de Guitarra but because it contains the theme of a Verdiales, a popular flamenco selection, often played at a flemenco gathering. The first 12 bars of the introduction is rather old-fashioned but from the 13th bar the tempo should be about ♩ =128 and played very staccato for the first 4 bars producing a tight rhythm as marked. The rest of this section should contain the same type of dance rhythm.

The tempo changes quite dramatically from the 'piu mosso' and is much faster until the end of the introduction. Then the theme begins in a heavily marked 6/8 or 3/4 rhythm marked at a tempo of ♩. = 84.

Be sure to establish the melody which, for the first 8 bars, is in the bass, changing round to the treble in the following 8 bars. You are sure to recognise the melody.

The variations are straightforward but must be played with precision in order to be effective, this could be quite a showpiece.

JULIO SAGRERAS Born Buenos Aires November 22nd 1879.
Pages 50 - 51

Julio Salavador Sagreras Ramerez was a musical prodigy who became a composer of many works for orchestra, piano, theatre and the guitar.

One of his most famous short pieces is El Colibri (The Hummingbird), which is often played as a showpiece by leading recitalists and should be in the repertoire of every guitarist as a practice piece for technical dexterity, and performance.

Julio Sagreras is also the author of an excellent guitar tutor.

This Sontina should be played at a brisk tempo of around ♪ = 120 similar in feel to a tango or habanera - eventually, that is, when the player has become familiar with the tune.

One could also play it at a slower tempo with the melody predominating by playing the melody notes with apoyando right hand picking: or practice at a faster tempo as a practice study. But which-ever, keep the arpeggios flowing.

8

FRANCISCO TARREGA (1852-1909)

There is a vast output from which to choose so I have taken three contrasting pieces not belonging to the obvious overdone "Rent-a-programmes".

Prelude No. 17 is an excellent practice or warming-up exercise starting at the bottom and climbing to the top note of the guitar: follow the fingering and the legatos and try to get there and back without a stop.

PAVANA is a mixture of Victorian and popular melody. The aportementos and grace notes are typical of Tarrega and his era, very much indulged in by his disciple Miguel Llobet. Although one should observe these slurs, they should be firm and definite not overdone and syrupy. The structure is A. B. A. with a four bar arpeggio after the middle eight bar [B] section returning to the original key of E from the usual key of B so watch out for the A sharps.

Allegro Brillante para Concierto is based on a violin solo by a famous french violinist and composer Jean Delphin Alard (1815-1888) which Tarrega turned into a popular showpiece for the guitar which is worth studying for many reasons - musical and technical. Take particular care in landing on the correct fingerboard positions, employing apoyando (i.e. down strokes) for the melody notes accompanied by flowing arpeggios.

The piece is still included in the guitar recitals and as I am writing this sentence I am listening to Turibio Santos performing it on the radio.

MIGUEL LLOBET was born in Barcelona on October 18th 1878, took up painting as a youngster, but eventually fell in love with the guitar.

He first studied with a modest teacher but by a fortunate coincidence was introduced to Francisco Tarrega whose pupil he became.

It is worth quoting Segovia's opinion of Llobet:

"Moreover, a teacher, Tarrega, had a following mainly made up of mediocre students with the exception of course of Miguel Llobet, who had a solid background, excellent technique and good judgement. He was a resourceful harmonist and also a fine transcriber".

Llobet spent a great deal of time in Argentina where he performed both as a soloist and with the young virtuoso Maria Luisa Anido to whom he dedicated this Prelude written for her in Barcelona on September 7th 1916.

He also arranged the two folk tunes which I have named: a) The Village Maiden and b) El Caballero. They have both the true spirit of the Argentine and sound as fresh today as when they were discovered.

EL NOY DE LA MARE (Catalan Folk Song)   Pages 59 - 60

This is a very beautiful tune and although uncomplicated is enriched by entrancing harmonies.

This version is one I learnt from the Spanish guitarist and teacher Jose Luis Gonzalez and it requires dexterity and independence of the left hand movement, not to mention large stretches.

In bar 7 you are required to hold the treble chord while changing the fingering of the bass note G. This is necessary in order to accomodate the G and F melody which follows. 5 bars from the end A, a large finger stretch is required in order to play the sixth string chord which contains open D. G. and B. strings but a fingered D on the first string, fingered E on the fifth string and G on the sixth.

Make sure the harmonies are clear in the last 2 bars. It is a most enjoyable piece to play both for the player and the listener.

GUARDAME LAS VACAS

LUYS DE NARVAEZ

Variation 1

Variation 2

CV

IV

III

Variation 3

SUITE PEGUEÑA
ESPANOLETA

GASPAR SANZ

rit. poco a poco

CANARIOS

GASPAR SANZ

PASSACALLE

GASPAR SANZ

18

LARGO

(from Concerto for Harpsichord No. 5)

J.S. BACH

Harm. 12

THE KING OF DENMARK'S GALLIARD

Transcribed from the lute tablature by Ivor Mairants

JOHN DOWLAND

6th to D

22

23

* 44 bars omitted.

FANTASIA

ALONSO MUDARRA

poco lento ma molto ritmico

CII

(Alternative fingering)

SUITE IN A MINOR

ROBERT DE VISEE

28

Menuet (2)

rit. last time

MENUET

(Opus 25)

FERNANDO SOR

ANDANTE LARGO

FERNANDO SOR

RONDO IN C

(Opus 22)

FERNANDO SOR

VARIATIONS ON AN ITALIAN AIR

MATTEO CARCASSI

THEME

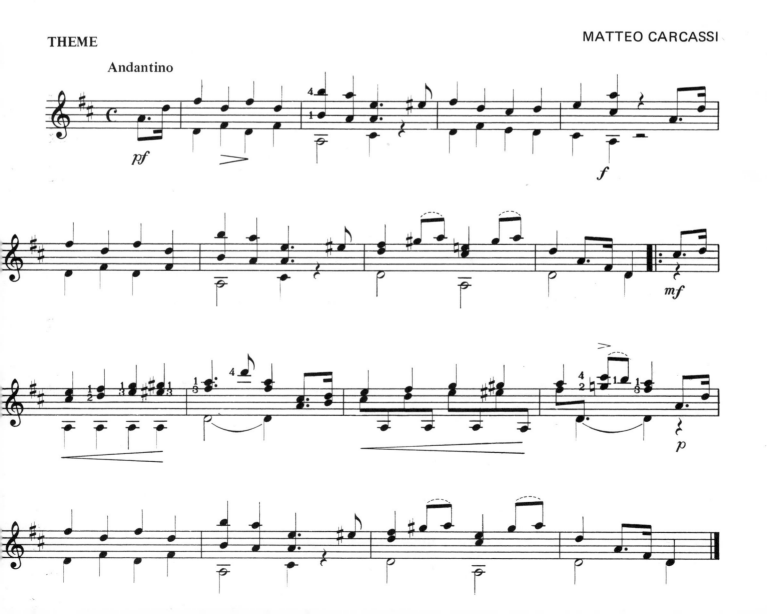

VARIATION 1

VARIATION 2

Légèrement

41

FANTASIA ON PUNTO DE LA HABANA

JULIAN GAVINADE DE ARCAS LACA

INTRODUCTION

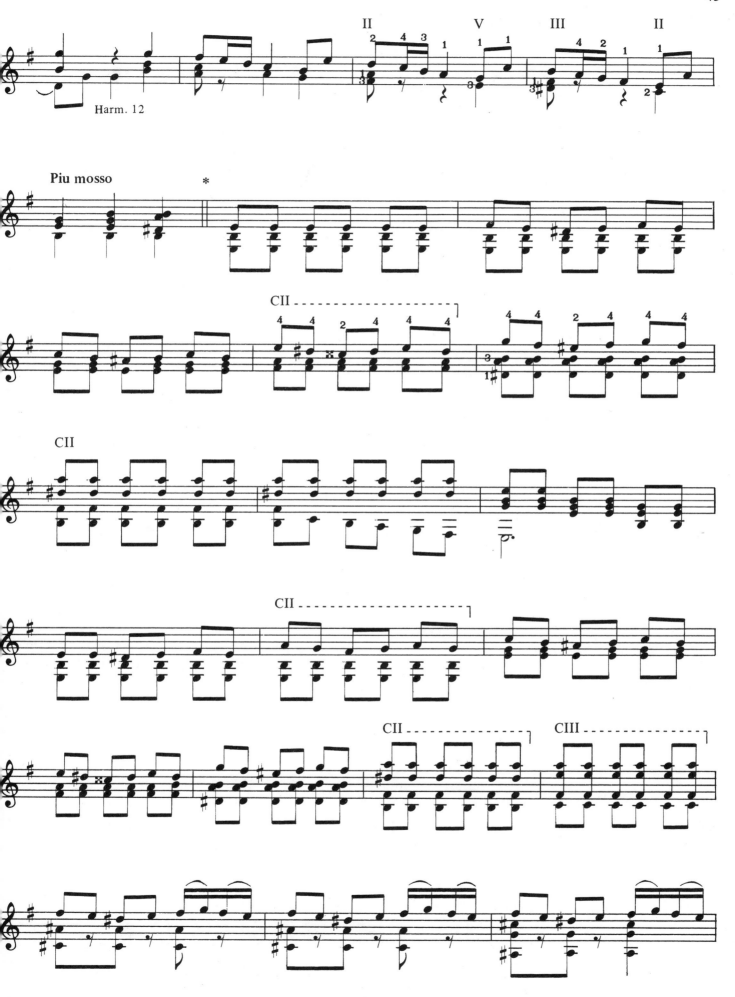

Harm. 12

Piu mosso

*

CII

CII

CII

CII

CII

CIII

Optional cut

44

THEME

♩. = 84

VARIATION 1

VARIATION 2

VARIATION 3

VARIATION 4

FINALE

SONATINA

(Estudio No. 1)

JULIO SAGRERA

51

PRELUDE NO. 17

FRANCISCO TARREGA

PAVANA

FRANCISCO TARREGA

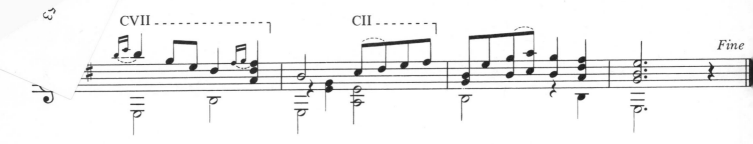

ALLEGRO BRILLIANTE

FRANCISCO TARREGA

PRELUDE FOR MARIA LUISA AWID

TWO ARGENTINIAN FOLK TUNES
THE VILLAGE MAIDEN

MIGUEL LLOBET

EL CABALLERO

MIGUEL LLOBET

EL NOY DE LA MARE

(A Catalan Folk Song)

Arr. **JOSE LUIS GONZALEZ**